T0380451

Foodie Lata

By Lata Talwar

This book is dedicated to my mum and dad, who have always believed in me, told me to aim high, and encouraged me to follow my dreams.

AuthorHouse™ UK
1663 Liberty Drive
Bloomington, IN 47403 USA
www.authorhouse.co.uk
Phone: 0800 047 8203 (Domestic TFN)
+44 1908 723714 (International)

Published by AuthorHouse 07/03/2019

ISBN: 978-1-7283-9034-5 (sc)
ISBN: 978-1-7283-9035-2 (e)

Print information available on the last page.

This book is printed on acid-free paper.

Editorial director: Victoria Munday
Design editor: Lucinda Hill
Design concept and layout: Energy Creative Ltd
Photo credit: AM Photography

authorHOUSE®

Content

Introduction

"Just add a bit of this, Lata, then add a bit of that."

My mother never used a recipe.

One of my earliest memories is hopping up on the kitchen worktop to watch her as she cooked. She produced amazing food for us all from the vast recipe repository in her mind – to her, cooking was as instinctive as breathing. As I grew up, she would spend hours in the kitchen cooking for us all, and I was usually to be found perched on top of the kitchen table, watching what she was doing. One of the first dishes I made was paneer pakora – a type of Indian snack – and seeing the joy on everyone's faces as they ate them is a memory I treasure.

My roots have strongly influenced what and how I cook. My upbringing has made me who I am today, and I'm eternally grateful to my parents for teaching me not only how to cook, but also all about my heritage. On our regular visits to Nani and Nana in India, I fell in love with an Indian street food called Pani Puri, which we used to eat in the street outside the cinema before going to watch the latest Bollywood film. They're still one of my favourite foods today. Visits to India took us all over the country staying with relatives. I still have the notebook which contains many original family recipes in Hindi, which I carefully copied from my cousins' cookery book over the course of a long hot summer.

Today, I cook for friends and family. I make an occasion out of every meal, carefully thinking about what dishes go together and considering how to serve each dish so it adds to the overall experience. It doesn't always need to be complicated – adding in new twists and flavours can be a gamechanger.

I hope you enjoy my recipes. They were created with love.

Happy cooking!

Love
Lata xx

Preparation & planning ahead

It's great to have a few items in the fridge so you're not always starting from scratch. There are a few basics I always make sure I have made up in the fridge, ready for when the urge to cook hits.

Ghee

I love ghee! Also known as clarified butter, it has many Ayurveda benefits and has a beautiful nutty flavour. It's always my preferred choice when cooking. You can store ghee for a long time, as long as you do not use any wet spoons in it, or get any water in it, so I always batch make my ghee. You will need a cheesecloth and a funnel to make this recipe.

2kg organic salted butter

1. Chop all the butter into small chunks and place in a heavy based pan. Let the butter melt slowly over a medium heat. Once melted, reduce the heat right down and leave to simmer for around 15 minutes. You'll notice some foam appearing and I remove this by running a small sieve over the top of the melted butter.

2. After 15 minutes, the milk solids should have separated, and you will see the milk solids suspended in the melted ghee. At this point, remove the pan from the heat.

3. Place the cheesecloth over the top of the funnel before putting the end of the funnel into an airtight jar. Pour the substance into the jar through the cheesecloth and funnel. After you finish pouring, remove the cheesecloth and dispose of the solids.

4. That's it, you have successfully made ghee! It does not need to be stored in the fridge, however you can keep in the fridge if you like.

Paneer

A soft cheese which doesn't melt, paneer is made by curdling milk. It's squeaky, fresh and incredibly versatile as well as being super tasty. Have your cheesecloth ready in a mixing bowl, ready for pouring. Once you've poured the mixture into the cheesecloth, you can tie the ends around a wooden spoon and use that to hang it over the bowl to drain.

4 litres full fat milk
3 tbsp lemon juice

1. Bring the milk to the boil in a large heavy based pan, stirring occasionally to ensure it does not burn. Allow to boil for a couple of minutes before reducing the heat.

2. Add the lemon juice and allow the mixture to simmer. Keep stirring, and you will notice the milk start to separate. When all the milk is separated, take the pan off the heat and drain the cheese into a cheesecloth.

3. Tie the cheesecloth and leave to hang over a bowl for around an hour. After an hour the cheese will have cooled off, so you can now retie the cheesecloth nice and tightly, twisting it to apply more pressure. I just do this onto the worktop with a heavy pan on top of the cheese in the muslin cloth. You can, however, put it on a plate if you wish.

4. Place a heavy object over the cheese as this will help it firm up and leave for around 6 hours on the side. Once firm, chop into cubes and store in the fridge. This should keep for 2-3 days in the fridge.

Ginger garlic paste

I use a 50/50 recipe for my ginger and garlic paste, as time goes on you may wish to alter the ratio if you prefer the taste of one over the other in cooking.

200g peeled garlic
200g fresh ginger root, peeled
1 tsp sea salt
100ml cold water

1. Add the garlic, ginger, salt and 50ml of the water into a blender and whizz until it reaches the desired consistency. If you would like it smoother, keep gradually adding water until it reaches your ideal consistency.

2. You can keep the paste in an airtight container in the fridge for around 2 weeks, or you can keep some in the fridge and put the rest into ice cube trays in the freezer and then just remove as required.

My spice box

Every Indian kitchen has its' own spice box, containing individual spices and personal blends. Mine is a kitchen essential. It's not only a way to keep my spices fresh so as not to lose flavour, but also means they are to hand when I need them at the right point during cooking.

When it comes to making the spice blends, if you don't have a spice grinder, use a pestle and mortar or a blender.

- Coriander powder

- Organic turmeric powder – said to have anti-inflammatory and medicinal properties, this has a bright yellow colour.

- Kashmiri chilli powder – this gives your recipes a subtle chilli flavour, rather than a fiery taste, whilst still retaining a vibrant red colour.

- Asafoetida powder – said to help with stomach problems when used in food daily, this has a strong potent smell.

- Cumin powder

- Cumin seeds

- Black cardamom pods

- Green cardamom pods

- Green cardamom powder

- Coriander seeds

- Cloves

- Mango powder

- Salt

- Chat masala – you can buy this, or you can make your own

- Garam masala – you can buy this, or you can make your own

Garam masala

150g cumin seeds
100g green cardamom seeds
50g black cardamom seeds
50g black peppercorns
50g coriander seeds
50g fennel seeds
25g cloves
75g bay leaves
3 cinnamon sticks

Chaat masala

2 tsp cumin seeds
1 tsp pomegranate seeds
½ tsp black peppercorns
1 tbsp mango powder
2 tsp black salt
1 tsp dried mint leaves
1 tsp carrom seeds (ajwain seeds)
1 tsp rock salt
1 tsp citric acid powder

1. The method for both these spice mixes is the same. Once done, fill up your spice box and use when you need to.

2. Dry roast all the whole ingredients in a pan over a medium heat for a few minutes.

3. In a coffee grinder, grind all the ingredients until powdered. You can use the mixes like this if you wish, but I like to sieve the powder to remove any larger solids.

Starters & street food

No street in India is complete without at least two carts offering scrumptious delights. The hidden gems of Indian cuisine, these stalls cook up delicious flavours in next to no time. Spicy aromas hang in the air, enticing you to try exciting new snacks. It's something you shouldn't miss out on, so that's why I've recreated my favourites here for you to try at home.

Pinwheel samosa

An elegant twist on the traditional samosa, these pretty pin wheels are ideal to serve as a party canape.

If you're in a rush, use shop bought puff pastry. Alternatively, try our delicious dough:

125g plain flour
¾ tsp salt
20g semolina
1 tsp onion seeds
2 tbsp sunflower oil, plus extra for drizzling
10ml cold milk
75ml water

For the filling

5 medium sized potatoes, peeled, boiled and diced
1 medium sized carrot, peeled, parboiled and diced
70g peas, boiled
1 tsp cumin seeds
1 tsp chilli powder
½ tsp ajwain seeds (also known as carrom seeds)
1 tsp coriander powder
¼ tsp asafoetida powder
1 tsp garam masala
1 tsp finely sliced coriander leaves
Salt to taste

1. First make your dough. In a large mixing bowl, sieve the flour, salt and semolina. Add the onion seeds, oil and milk.

2. Slowly add the water, mixing with a wooden spoon and then your hands, until a soft, pliable dough forms. Cover the dough and leave to rest for 2 hours. While the dough is resting, add all of the filling ingredients into a bowl, mix well and set aside.

3. When you're ready to cook these, preheat your oven to 180°C, 350°F, or gas mark 4.

4. When the dough has rested, knead and roll out into a large rectangle. You don't want the dough to be too thick – you're aiming for slightly thicker than a chapatti. If you find it easier, you can always cut the dough into smaller rectangles.

5. Once rolled out, spread the filling across the dough before rolling the dough and filling into a swiss roll shape and sealing the dough with water. Trim the ends of the roll before slicing the roll into 3 to 5 cm slices. Place the circles onto a greased baking tray, making sure they don't touch.

6. Drizzle a little oil over them and bake for 20 mins until crisp and nicely browned.

Kebabs

Indian kebabs are a vital part of parties and are fabulous served with chutneys or dipped into raita. Formed into chunky sausages around skewers and then baked, these scrumptious skewers are packed full of flavour. The key to a successful kebab is to get as much moisture out of the onion as you can, as doing this helps to prevent the kebab falling apart when cooking. My top tip? If you soak your wooden skewers in water before use, you'll avoid them burning.

Lamb kebabs

One of the first recipes I learned to cook, these traditional kebabs provide a great starter or an easy midweek meal. Don't shape them too thinly, you're aiming for around 10cm length and 3cm width.

500g minced lamb
1 finely diced onion
1 tsp finely sliced ginger
20g roughly sliced leaves mint leaves
20g roughly sliced coriander leaves
1 green chilli, seeds removed, finely sliced
1 tsp coriander powder
1 tsp cumin powder
¼ tsp asafoetida
Salt to taste
Wooden skewers
Wedge of lemon and chaat masala to garnish

1. Place the onion into a muslin cloth and squeeze as much liquid out as you can.

2. In a large mixing bowl, kneed the minced lamb with all the spices and onions for around 5 minutes until fully blended. Once mixed, take a handful of lamb and create a sausage-shaped kebab around each skewer. When all your skewers are made, place in the fridge for around 2 hours before cooking.

3. To bake, pre-heat your oven to 180°C, 350°F, or gas mark 4 and once at temperature pop the skewers in for around 20 minutes. Once cooked through, remove from the oven and sprinkle some chaat masala over them before serving with a wedge of lemon.

Vegetable kebab

You can use almost any vegetable in a kebab – it's a great way to try out new ingredients. This recipe will transform even the humblest of vegetables into a flavoursome, fabulous starter!

Quarter of a finely sliced onion
1 inch fresh ginger root, peeled and finely sliced into sticks
1 finely sliced green chilli, seeds included
2 tbsp roasted gram flour (you can quickly roast the flour in a pan or oven until lightly browned)
1 peeled and grated raw carrot
50g boiled kidney beans
70g boiled peas
4 peeled and boiled potatoes
2 tbsp almond flour
1 tbsp cornflour
1 tsp Kashmiri red chilli powder
1 tsp turmeric
1 tsp coriander powder
1 tsp garam masala
1 tsp finely sliced mint leaves
1 tsp sliced coriander leaves
1 slice of bread, ground into breadcrumbs
½ tsp chaat masala
12 wooden skewers, soaked in water

1. Pre-heat your oven to 180°C, 350°F, or gas mark 4.

2. Place all the ingredients into a large mixing bowl and, using your hands, mix together and form into a dough. Pinch off small amounts and make into balls. If it needs a little liquid to keep them together, try adding a little oil.

3. Mould the mixture onto the skewers as above and place on a greased oven tray. You can bake these immediately if you wish, or place in the fridge until you're ready to cook them.

4. Bake for around 10 minutes, before turning the skewers over for a further 5 minutes.

5. Serve with a salad, accompanied by chutney.

Tandoori bases

A tandoor is generally used to cook these recipes, however
nowadays we can use the oven to do this!

Red tandoori

Red tandoori base

Don't limit this to using it when you make a curry – try it out on other things! Rub it on meat, add it to paneer or tofu, or toss root vegetables in it before roasting them. Try mixing it with plain yogurt to marinade meat or fish before grilling. Using Greek yogurt ensures there isn't too much liquid in the marinade.

2 tbsp ginger and garlic paste
4 tsp Kashmiri red chilli powder
8 tbsp thick Greek yogurt
1 tsp ghee
¼ tsp turmeric
½ tsp mango powder
½ tsp carom seeds
1½ tbsp gram flour
½ tsp chat masala
1 tsp garam masala
1 tsp crushed kasuri methi (dried fenugreek leaves)
Salt to taste
Lemon wedge to garnish
Chat masala for seasoning

1. Heat the ghee in a pan then add the carom seeds. Allow the seeds to sizzle and, once sizzling, add in the gram flour. You need to roast the gram flour until it changes colour, before adding the turmeric and methi. Stir and cook for 1 minute to release the spice flavours before removing from the heat and transferring to a large mixing bowl.

2. Add the Greek yogurt into the same mixing bowl. Add the ginger, garlic paste, Kashmiri chilli powder, chat masala, garam masala, mango powder and salt. Whisk the mixture till entirely blended.

3. Now add your meat or vegetables to the mixture.

4. Cover and place the bowl in the fridge for at least an hour. I love making this mixture in the morning, so when I come home from work I can simply place the tray into the oven.

Red chicken tandoori

Tandoori chicken is named after the traditional bell-shaped tandoor clay oven which is also used to make naan bread. Thankfully, you don't need a tandoor oven to make tandoori chicken – either barbeque it or grill it.

12 chicken drumsticks
1 portion tandoori base, as above
½ tsp beetroot powder (you can use food colouring if you want to create a brighter tandoori colour)
Salt for seasoning

1. Remove the skin from the drumsticks and score with a knife. This enables the flavour to penetrate through the meat. Add the chicken drumsticks to the tandoori base mixture. Make sure the chicken is covered in the sauce and massage the base mixture into it.

2. Cover the chicken mixture and place in the fridge for a minimum of 2 hours. The longer you leave it, the better – so aim for 8 hours if you can.

3. Using a barbecue to cook these gives the drumsticks that really smoky flavour, or you can cook them in the oven.

4. Pre-heat your oven to 180°C, 350°F, or gas mark 4 and place a grill tray over a baking dish. Baking them in this way prevents them from going soggy – you want the crispness of a grill without being smothered in sauce. Spread your marinated drumsticks on the tray and pop in the oven.

5. Cook the chicken for around 20 to 25 minutes depending on the size of your drumsticks. Once the chicken is cooked with the juices running clear, remove from the grill and place on your serving dish. Serve with a wedge of lemon, sprinkle some chat masala over it, serve with some mint yogurt chutney.

Red broccoli tandoori

The kick of tandoori spices lends itself well to vegetables. Here we've used it to make a broccoli curry, but this is a great base for experimenting with all sorts of vegetables. The beetroot powder is optional, and I use it instead of food colouring. I add it to create more of the traditional 'tandoori' colour.

1 head of broccoli, cut into florets
1 portion tandoori base, as above
½ tsp beetroot powder
Salt to taste

1. Add the broccoli florets to the tandoori base mixture, making sure the broccoli is fully coated.

2. Cover and pop into the fridge for a minimum of 2 hours – the longer you leave this, the better it is, so aim for 8 hours.

3. Pre-heat your oven to 180°C, 350°F, or gas mark 4. Place a grill tray on top of your oven tray, as if you bake it in the tandoori mixture the vegetables will be in too much liquid and go soggy.

4. Cook the broccoli for around 20 to 25 minutes. Once cooked, serve with a wedge of lemon, sprinkle some chat masala over it, or with some mint yogurt chutney.

Hari tandoori

Hari tandoori paste

30g coriander leaves
15g mint leaves
Handful of spinach leaves
2 tsp kasoori methi (dried fenugreek leaves)
5 tbsp of Greek yogurt
2 tsp roasted gram flour
1 tsp cumin powder
Salt to taste
1 tsp chat masala
½ tsp turmeric powder
½ tsp mango powder
½ tsp garam masala
½ tsp of asafoetida

1. In a spice grinder, grind the coriander leaves, mint leaves, spinach leaves, kasoori methi with one teaspoon of the yogurt. It should form a paste, however, if you feel it needs grinding more, add some more yogurt and continue to grind.

2. Place the remaining yogurt and ground mixture into a mixing bowl and whisk until it is incorporated. Add the gram flour, cumin powder, salt, chat masala, turmeric powder, mango powder, garam masala and asafoetida before mixing well.

3. Add your chosen vegetables or meat into the mixture and marinate for a minimum of 2 hours (ideally 8 hours if you have the time).

4. Once marinated, cook the vegetables or meat in the oven on a raised grill tray for the desired time for the vegetables or meat.

Hari paneer tikka

1 portion hari tandoori paste, as above
1 tsp chaat masala
1 tsp ginger paste
1 green chilli
20 large chunks of paneer
Salt to taste
Lemon wedge and chaat masala to garnish
Cocktail sticks

1. Put 3 tbsp of the hari tandoori paste, the chaat masala, ginger paste and 1 green chilli into a blender and blend until smooth. It is up to you whether you wish to remove the seeds from the chilli to make it less spicy.

2. Cut a slit into each paneer chunk, you want them to still stay together so be sure not to go all the way through.

3. Fill the slits in the paneer with the paste, and once they're filled put a cocktail stick through them to keep them together.

4. Place the paneer into a dish and marinate them in the rest of the hari tandoori paste.

5. Pop them in the fridge an let them rest for a minimum of 2 hours, if you would like a stronger flavour marinate them for around 8 hours.

6. Once marinated it's up to you how you cook the paneer. You can either barbecue them for a smokier flavour, or cook them in the oven.

7. If you opt for the oven option, pre-heat your oven to 180°C, 350°F, or gas mark 4 and put the paneer onto a grill tray. The grill tray will catch all of the liquid without drowning the paneer.

8. Once you've placed them on the tray, baste them with the leftover paste.

9. Cook the paneer for around 15 minutes and then grill for 5 minutes to crisp them up.

10. Once cooked, put them into a serving dish and decorate with a wedge of lemon and sprinkle over some chaat masala. The paneer chunks go very well with a mint yoghurt chutney!

Hari lamb chops

12 lamb chops
1 portion of hari tandoori paste
Salt to taste
Lemon wedge and chaat masala to garnish

1. Score the chops with a knife to allow the flavours to penetrate the meat. Add the chops to the hari tandoori paste and massage the paste into the chops. Cover the bowl and pop into the fridge for a minimum of 2 hours, for a more marinated chop I'd recommend leaving them in the fridge for around 8 hours.

2. You can either put the chops on the barbecue to get a really smoky flavour, or you can cook them in the oven. If you opt for the oven, pre-heat your oven to 180°C, 350°F, or gas mark 4.

3. I like to sear my chops before I put them in the oven, but this is optional. If you would like to sear the chops, put the chops into a grill pan and sear until you get the grilled lines on the chops.

4. Now put the chops onto a grill tray and baste with the hari tandoori paste that they marinated in. The grill tray is important as it allows the liquid to run beneath the chops.

5. Cook the chops in the oven for around 15 minutes. The exact cooking time depends on the size of the chops, so leave them in for a little longer if they're on the large side.

6. Once cooked, transfer to a serving dish and garnish with a wedge of lemon and a sprinkle of chat masala. These chops go really well with a mint yoghurt chutney.

Curries

The classic dish of India, curries vary wildly depending on the region and even the kitchen they come from. Once you've mastered curry bases you can use them in a variety of ways to add flavour, from using them as a rub to marinade meat or adding them to roast vegetables to impart the flavour you want. Make them in advance and store them in airtight containers to keep them fresh – these take the worry out of making curry at home, meaning you don't need to resort to ordering a takeaway!

Curry bases

Once you're confident in making these, you can use them in many different ways to create many fabulous dishes. You'll find as time goes on that you won't need to measure ingredients but will go by what the base looks like and how it tastes. Feel free to tweak the flavour balance until it makes your tastebuds happy!

Onion & tomato tadka

Onion & tomato tadka base

Tadka is a gravy or a paste used in almost all curry based Indian recipes. It's an essential part of Indian cooking and brings with it bags of flavour. I always have a batch in the fridge ready to use, and usually some in the freezer. It's incredibly adaptable – you can even cook it separately and then mix it with vegetables for a quick guest-ready dish.

2 tbsp ghee
1 tsp cumin seeds
4 large sliced onions
1 tsp ginger and garlic paste
1 tsp turmeric
6 tomatoes, diced
2 tsp coriander powder
1 tsp chilli powder
2 tsp garam masala
Salt to taste

1. Add the ghee into a large heavy based pan and heat until melted. Add the cumin seeds and allow to sizzle but be careful not to burn them.

2. After a minute or so add the onions and keep stirring until they soften, then add the ginger and garlic pastes and allow to cook for 2 to 3 minutes.

3. Add the turmeric powder and mix thoroughly before adding the tomatoes and salt. If the tomato mixture begins to stick add a little water. Cook for 10 minutes then stir in the coriander powder, chilli powder and garam masala.

4. When the oil rises and separates from the mixture, remove from the heat.

Allow the mixture to cool and either store in the fridge or freezer for future use

Chicken curry

A common delicacy in the Indian subcontinent, my chicken curry is incredibly easy to make, especially if you've a portion of tadka base already in the fridge or freezer.

1 portion tomato and onion tadka base
500g chicken breast, raw, diced into large chunks
240ml boiling water
Salt to taste
Finely sliced coriander to garnish

1. Add the tomato and onion tadka base to a large heavy pan and bring to a simmer, then add the chicken to the pan. Add the cup of water into the pan and stir until the mixture and water is blended into the tadka.

2. Reduce the heat to a gentle simmer and cover, allowing it to slow cook.

3. Leave this for around 20 minutes.

4. After around 20 minutes remove the lid and check whether you think it is too watery or whether it needs more water adding.

5. Cook for a further 20 minutes, stirring occasionally.

6. The curry should leave some residue on the back of a spoon if it is the right consistency.

7. Once you have reached the right consistency, check the curry is to your taste and add some more salt or chilli if you feel it is required.

8. Take the curry off the hob, place into a serving dish and add some coriander over the top for decoration.

Lamb curry

500g lamb chunks
30g yogurt
1 tsp garam masala
Pinch of turmeric powder
Pinch of asafoetida
Pinch of chilli powder

Curry:

Splash of oil
2 green crushed cardamom
2 black crushed cardamom pieces
2 bay leaves
1 cinnamon stick
1 tsp crushed fennel seeds
1 portion of tomato and onion tadka base
1 sliced chilli
225ml boiling water
Salt to taste

Dressing:

Yogurt
Chopped coriander

1. Begin by scoring the lamb so that it can soak up the marinade and absorb the flavours.

2. In a large bowl, mix the lamb, yogurt, garam masala, turmeric powder, asafoetida and chilli powder.

3. Once it is all mixed, leave for as long as possible to marinate. Overnight is ideal, or you can just marinate it for 4 hours if you're short of time.

4. Add a splash of oil to a large heavy based pan, and heat through. Add the green and black cardamom, cloves, bay leaves, cinnamon stick and the fennel seeds. Let this simmer for a few minutes.

5. Next, add the tomato and onion tadka base to the pan, and bring to the boil.

6. Once boiling, leave for a couple of minutes, before adding the marinated lamb along with the leftover marinade to the pan.

7. Heat through until hot, then add the boiling water and mix until the water and marinade are blended.

8. Bring the mixture to the boil, then cover and reduce the heat in order to allow the curry to slow cook.

9. After 20 minutes, remove the cover and check to see whether the curry requires any more water. Add a splash if required to prevent the curry from sticking. The sauce should be thick enough to cover the back of a spoon.

10. Once you have checked, continue to cook for another 20 minutes, stirring occasionally.

Vegetable sabzi

1 tbsp ghee
1 tsp cumin seeds
1/2 a cauliflower head, cut into florets
150g peas
30g finely sliced spinach
1 diced carrot
4 tbsp onion and tomato tadka base
Salt to taste
Fresh coriander to garnish

1. In a medium, heavy based pan, heat the ghee until melted and add the cumin seeds. Allow these to sizzle slightly before adding the cauliflower and carrots. Sauté until slightly soft then add the peas and spinach.

2. Mix well before adding the tomato and onion tadka base. Heat through and stir until blended before bringing to the boil, then reduce the heat. Allowing it to slow cook for 15 minutes, stirring so it doesn't stick at this stage.

3. Check for seasoning to see if it requires any more salt or chilli.

4. Take the curry off the heat, before sprinkling some coriander over the top for decoration.

Butter masala

Butter masala base

12 cashews
1 tsp ghee
2 black cardamom seeds, ground
2 green cardamom seeds, ground
1 sliced green chilli, seeds included
1 portion onion and tomato tadka
1 tsp garam masala
½ tsp asafoetida
Salt to taste
Single cream and a handful of finely sliced coriander leaves to garnish

1. Soak the cashews in hot water for 30 minutes.

2. Meanwhile, add the ghee, cardamom and chilli into a large pan. Let it sizzle for a minute over a medium heat in order to release the flavours, before adding the tomato onion tadka base and gently bringing to the boil.

3. Whilst the tadka base is coming to the boil, blend the soaking cashews with a few teaspoons of the water they have soaked in until it turns into a smooth paste. Do this by adding a teaspoon at a time until it reaches a thick consistency.

4. Add the paste to the masala, stirring well, and continue to cook until you see the colour change. Once the colour has changed to a deep red, add all your dry spices and let them cook for a few minutes before stirring. Once thoroughly incorporated, transfer the mixture into the blender and add some water to top the masala off. Blend until it becomes a smooth paste.

5. Place the blended paste back into the pan and cook it off over a medium heat. Whilst you are cooking you will notice the colour changing to a deeper red. You'll need to keep stirring the mixture to prevent it from sticking.

6. Add a little water to the mixture to loosen it and stir through.

7. If you have decided to add some meat or vegetable chunks, add them now. Brown any meat first in a separate pan over a high heat, using a teaspoonful of ghee, before adding to the curry. If using paneer or vegetables, add them directly to the curry.

8. Cover the pan, reduce the heat down to low and cook the mixture for around 20 minutes if you added vegetables, or longer if you added meat. Once cooked, remove the lid and stir through before transferring to a serving dish. Use the cream to create a swirl over the top before decorating with coriander.

Butter chicken

There's an ongoing debate about how this dish first came into existence. Some say that it was invented when dry tandoori chicken was put into a spicy, creamy sauce to give it moisture, before having butter added. Others that the inclusion of butter or ghee into the browning of the meat. Either way, it tastes delicious and is one of the first dishes I recommend when I'm asked for a recipe by folk who want to try making Indian food at home for the first time.

12 cashews
1 tsp ghee
2 black cardamom seeds, ground
2 green cardamom seeds, ground
1 chilli, sliced
600g chicken breast, diced
1 portion of tomato onion masala base
1 tsp garam masala
½ tsp asafoetida
Salt to taste
Cream and finely sliced coriander to garnish

1. Put the cashews into hot water to soak for 30 minutes.

2. Meanwhile, add the ghee, cardamom and chilli into a large pan. Let it sizzle for a minute in order to release the flavours.

3. Add the chicken chunks into the sizzling pan and let them cook for a few minutes.

4. Once the chicken has cooked for a few minutes, add the tomato onion masala base and heat through until boiling.

5. As the masala base is coming to the boil, blend the soaking cashews with some of the water they have been soaking in, until it forms a smooth paste.

6. Add the paste to the masala and then continue to cook until you see the colour change.

7. Once the colour has changed add all your dry spices and let them cook for a few minutes. After they have cooked for a few minutes stir the ingredients to ensure it is all mixed through.

8. Once mixed add the mixture into the blender and add some water to top the masala off. Blend until it becomes a smooth paste.

9. Once fully blended add the paste you have blended back into the pan and cook it off. Whilst you are cooking you will notice the colour changing, keep stirring the mixture so it does not stick.

10. Add a little water to the mixture and stir through.

11. Cover the pan, reduce the heat down and cook the mixture for around 20 minutes.

12. After 20 minutes, remove the lid and stir through.

13. Once stirred, add the butter chicken to a serving dish. Use the cream to create a swirl over the top and decorate with finely sliced coriander.

Butter paneer

One of the most popular paneer recipes in Indian cuisine, this combines spiciness with creaminess and the result is just…. mmm mmm divine!

12 cashews
1 tsp ghee
2 black cardamom seeds, ground
2 green cardamom seeds, ground
1 chilli, sliced
1 portion tomato onion masala base
1 tsp garam masala
½ tsp asafoetida
20 chunks of paneer, cut into 5cm cubes
Salt, as required
Garnish
Cream and finely sliced coriander to garnish

1. Soak the cashews in hot water for 30 minutes.

2. Whilst the cashews are soaking, add the ghee, cardamom and chilli into the pan and let them sizzle for a few minutes to release the flavours. Add the tomato onion masala base to the pan and heat through until it is boiling.

3. Meanwhile, blend the cashews, along with some of the water that they have been soaking in, until they turn into a smooth paste. Add the cashew paste to the masala and cook until you notice a colour change. Add all your dry spices and let them cook for a few minutes before stirring thoroughly.

4. Once stirred, add the mixture back into the blender and add some water to top the masala off. Blend the mixture until it turns into a smooth paste. Add the paste back into the pan and cook it off.

5. As the mixture cooks you will notice the colour changing, make sure you keep stirring it so that it does not stick. Add the paneer chunks and stir through.

6. Pour in a little water, stir through and then cover the pan. Reduce the heat down and cook the curry for around 20 minutes.

7. Remove the lid and stir through.

8. Add the butter paneer to a serving dish and use the cream to create a swirl over the top, before decorating with finely sliced coriander.

Palak

Palak base

This north Indian recipe offers something a bit different.

650g spinach leaves
4 tbsp coriander leaves
1 tbsp ghee
2 tsp cumin seeds
1 sliced onion
1 deseeded and finely sliced green chilli
1 tbsp garlic and ginger paste
1 tbsp coriander powder
1 tsp turmeric
1 tsp Kashmiri chilli powder
1 tsp cumin powder
1 tbsp garam masala
1 tbsp yogurt
1 tsp asafoetida
1 tbsp sliced garlic
½ tsp mango powder
Salt to taste

1. Blanch the spinach leaves in hot water, then place in a blender with the coriander leaves and pulse until they form a paste. Once blended, move the paste to one side.

2. Melt the ghee over a medium heat in a heavy based pan, before adding the cumin seeds and allowing to simmer for a minute or so. Then add the onion and chilli and cook until the onion is soft.

3. Add the garlic, ginger paste, coriander powder, turmeric, chilli powder, cumin powder, mango powder, asafoetida and garam masala and stir. Keep stirring until you begin to see the oil rise. If the spices start to stick, add a little water.

4. Add the yogurt, stir and cook for a few minutes, before adding the spinach paste and bringing to the boil for 5 to 10 minutes. Add salt to taste. Remove from the heat and there you have it, a base for any spinach dish which you can add to with chicken, paneer or any vegetables!

Palak chicken

12 chicken legs
1 tbsp yogurt
½ tsp turmeric
½ tsp Kashmiri red chilli
1 tbsp ghee
1 portion of palak base
Julienned ginger and finely shredded coriander to garnish

1. Score the chicken legs. Scoring the chicken legs allows the meat to soak up all the flavours and produces a more tender dish.

2. Add the chicken legs to a large bowl along with the yogurt, turmeric and red chilli and then stir.

3. Once mixed, cover the bowl and then pop it into the fridge for around 8 hours to marinate.

4. Once marinated, heat the ghee in a large pan and then add the chicken mixture, then cook for 5 minutes.

5. After 5 minutes, add the palak base to the pan and bring to the boil.

6. Once boiling add a couple of tablespoons of water, cover and simmer for 20 minutes.

7. After 20 minutes, remove from the heat and serve garnished with fresh ginger and coriander.

Palak sweetcorn

1 tbsp ghee
500g cubed paneer chunks
1 portion of palak base
1 drained tin of sweetcorn
Julienned ginger and finely shredded coriander to garnish

1. Melt the ghee in a large pan, then add the paneer chunks and stir until the paneer starts to brown slightly. Add the palak base and the sweetcorn and bring to the boil.

2. Once boiling, add a couple of tablespoons of water before covering and leaving to simmer for 20 minutes.

3. Remove the pan from the heat and serve, garnishing the dish with the ginger and coriander.

Dals

Feel good dal tadka

One of the most popular dishes ordered in Indian restaurants, this is a mouth-watering lentil dish which gets its flavour from aromatic tempering. I love eating dal with rice or as a soup – I'd go so far as to say it's a a necessity in my home life and my favourite 'go to' feel good food item. As it contains lots of vital vitamins, it is the ideal dish for making when you're under the weather and need a boost.

300g toor dal (pigeon peas)
1 tsp turmeric
Pinch of salt
Masala
1 tbsp ghee
2 tsp cumin seeds
2 tsp sliced ginger
1 tsp finely sliced garlic
1 dry red chilli

1 green chilli, cut in half and deseeded
1 sliced onion
3 medium tomatoes, skinned and diced
1 tsp Kashmiri red chilli powder
2 tsp garam masala
½ tsp asafoetida
Salt to taste
1 tsp coriander leaves, finely sliced and
½ tsp of ghee to garnish

1. Put the toor dal into a large bowl and rinse, before adding around 750ml water over the lentils. Make sure they are all soaking in the water, then add the turmeric and a pinch of salt. Mix and leave to soak for 2 hours.

2. After two hours, transfer the lentils and water into a large pan, and boil them for around 20 to 30 minutes on a medium heat.

3. Once boiled, remove a couple of lentils from the pan and check they are cooked. You can do this by squeezing them – they should be nice and soft. If they are not ready, keep them on the heat and retest every 5 minutes until they are.

4. Once the lentils are cooked, remove the foam from the top of the water by skimming with a sieve, then remove the lentils from the heat.

5. In a separate pan, simmer the ghee, cumin seeds, ginger, dry red chilli and the green chilli for 2 to 3 minutes. Then add the onion into the pan, cooking gently until it turns translucent and has slightly browned.

6. Add the tomatoes and cook for around 5 to 10 minutes, until the tomatoes have softened. Then add all the red chilli powder, garam masala and asafoetida. Let this cook for a few minutes, but make sure you stir the mixture continuously to avoid sticking.

7. Now add the boiled dal and stir through, then add around 200ml of water to the pan, and salt to taste.

8. Bring the mixture to the boil and then reduce the heat before leaving to simmer for 10 minutes.

9. Put the dal in a serving dish, garnishing with the coriander leaves and a little ghee.

Dal makhani

A fabulous dish from the Punjab region, this slow cooked lentil dish is in a league of its own. Traditionally served at celebrations including weddings, it's loaded with flavour.

250g whole urad dal
50g chana dal
100g kidney beans
1 tbsp ghee
1 tsp cumin seeds
1 green chilli, split in half
2 crushed black cardamom
2 crushed green cardamom

2 bay leaves
1 tbsp of sliced ginger and garlic
2 sliced onions
3 medium sliced tomatoes
2 tsp garam masala
2 tbsp cream
Salt to taste
Cream to garnish

1. Rinse the urad dal, chana dal and kidney beans before soaking overnight in 750ml of water.

2. In the morning, drain the lentils and add them to a large pan with 1 litre of water.

3. Bring the pan to the boil, then allow to simmer for 45 minutes.

4. After 45 minutes, check the lentils by squeezing a couple to see if they are cooked. If the lentils are still hard, keep them boiling and check every five minutes.

5. In a separate pan, melt the ghee then add the cumin seeds, green chilli, black and green cardamoms, bay leaves, ginger and garlic and let this sizzle for 2 minutes before adding the onions.

6. Once the onions are translucent and starting to brown, add the tomatoes and keep stirring for around 2 minutes.

7. Once soft the tomatoes are soft, add the garam masala.

8. Whilst this is bubbling away, drain the water from the lentils into a bowl, keeping the water to one side to use later.

9. Add the lentils into the masala base and cook for around 5 minutes before adding the leftover water and salt. Leave to simmer for around 25-30 minutes.

10. Stir in the cream and allow to cook for a further 5 minutes.

11. Take the dal off the heat and it is ready to serve. Garnish with a swirl of cream and enjoy with rice or chapatis.

Sides and salads

Indian side dishes are what turns a meal into a feast. No dinner table is complete without at least two side dishes which highlight and compliment the main curry. These are my tasty versions of the popular side dishes and salads which will take your meal from the ordinary to the extraordinary.

Cumin potatoes

Delicious either hot or cold, you can enjoy this alongside a curry or with another type of cuisine — it's very easy to prepare, yet tastes like you've spent hours in the kitchen.

1 tbsp ghee
1 tbsp cumin seeds
1 inch finely sliced fresh ginger, julienned if possible
1/2 tsp asafoetida powder
1 tsp turmeric powder
½ tsp garam masala
1/2 tsp mango powder
1 tsp coriander powder
4 boiled potatoes, cubed
Finely sliced coriander and 1 inch of finely sliced ginger, julienned if possible to garnish

1. Heat the ghee and cumin seeds in a pan. Let them sizzle for a little while and then add ginger, along with the dry spices. Allow to cook slightly — you'll be able to smell the flavours of the spices being released as they heat through.

2. Add the boiled potatoes and thoroughly mix to coat all the potatoes in the masala.

3. Once hot, take off the heat and place into a serving dish.

4. Garnish with coriander and ginger before serving.

Kachumber salad

A fresh and light vegetable salad which balances a curry without overwhelming it. This colourful and lightly spiced salad makes an excellent side dish.

1 red onion, diced
1 cucumber, diced
3 tomatoes, diced
5 red radishes, diced (any radish can be used)
1 green chilli, seeds removed and finely sliced
2 tbsp roughly sliced coriander
1 tbsp pomegranate seeds

Dressing

2 tbsp lemon juice
½ tsp red chilli powder
1 tsp chaat masala

1. Mix all of the dressing ingredients in a large bowl.

2. Add all the salad ingredients to the bowl and mix thoroughly so the salad is coated in the dressing.

3. Leave to soak for 30 minutes.

4. Serve and enjoy!

Pilau rice

An essential element to any curry feast which is incredibly easy to make – once you know how! I always work with cups in rice as I find it easier to measure. As long as you stick to a 1:1.5 ratio for rice to water, you can achieve whatever quantity of rice is desired.

1 cup basmati rice
1.5 cups water
1 tbsp ghee
1 tsp cumin seeds
2 cloves
1 black cardamom, crushed
1 bay leaf
1 tsp garam masala
1 onion, sliced
1 tsp ginger, julienned
1 potato, boiled and chopped
1 chopped carrot
2-3 florets of cauliflower, chopped
Salt to taste

1. Wash the rice in a bowl until the water runs clear. Drain and add the 1.5 cups of water and leave to soak for an hour.

2. In a large pan, melt the ghee before adding the cumin seeds, ginger, cloves, cardamom and bay leaf. Keep stirring for a minute or so. You will be able to smell the spices as they heat through.

3. Now add the sliced onion and cook until translucent. Then reduce the heat and allow the onions to brown. This will also give your rice a lovely brown colour. Once cooked, add the garam masala, carrot, cauliflower and potato and simmer for around 3 minutes.

4. If you prefer to cook your rice in a rice cooker, use it for the next stage. If you'd rather use a pan, add the salt, rice and the water from the rice into the pan and stir before bringing to the boil. Once boiling, turn the heat to low, cover with a lid and cook for 8 minutes.

5. Once it has been around 8 minutes, check whether the rice is cooked. Then take the rice off the heat, cover with a tea towel and put the lid back on, letting the steam do the rest of the cooking.

6. You can serve the rice along with any curry, with plain yogurt or on its own. Alternatively, try adding in cooked meat or fish instead of or as well as the vegetables.

Raita

One of the classic Indian side dishes, this takes the heat out of your curries and is perfect as a dip.

250g yogurt
2 tbsp milk
½ tsp coriander powder
Salt to taste
1 tsp cumin powder
1 small cucumber, grated
¼ onion, diced
1 small tomato, diced
Roasted cumin seeds and diced cucumber to garnish

1. Whisk the yogurt, milk, coriander powder, salt and cumin powder together.

2. Once thoroughly mixed, add the cucumber, onion, tomato and stir. If it is too thick, add a little more milk.

3. Transfer to a serving dish and garnish with some diced cucumber and roasted cumin seeds.

4. Keep in the fridge until you are ready to serve.

Mint chutney

This is my favourite chutney to keep in the fridge. It goes wonderfully well with many dishes, cooling and complementing curries.

100g coriander leaves
50 g mint leaves
2 tbsp ginger garlic paste
1 tsp salt
1 tsp sugar
1 tsp lemon juice
1 green chilli
1 tbsp water

1. Place all the ingredients into a blender and whizz until smooth. It will turn into a beautiful green chutney.

If you want to make mint yogurt chutney, simply mix a tablespoon of the mint chutney with a tablespoon of yogurt.

Mango pickle

4 green mangoes, sçkinned, destoned and diced
1 alphonso mango, skinned, destoned and diced
1 apple, skinned, cored and diced
1 tbsp white vinegar
1 tsp salt
2 tsp turmeric powder
The juice of 2 limes
1 tsp mango powder
2 tbsp sugar
2 crushed garlic cloves
1 tsp onion seeds
2 tbsp ghee
2 tsp cumin seeds
1 tsp red chilli powder

1. Place the apple, mangoes, white vinegar, salt and turmeric in a large jar, put the lid on and leave to soak for 24 hours.

2. Add the lime juice, mango powder, sugar, crushed garlic and onion seeds, replace the lid, and shake.

3. Melt the ghee in a pan then add the cumin seeds and chilli powder and allow to sizzle, releasing the flavours. Cool, then add the ghee, cumin seed and chilli powder mixture to the jar and shake well.

4. Leave the pickle for 3 days before consuming. Once opened, keep in the fridge.

Garlic naan bread

Quick and easy to make, enjoy these warm with your favourite curry. Fluffy and fragrant, these oven baked flatbreads are found in varying forms in many different cuisines.

400ml hot water
1 tsp salt
2 tsp sugar
1 tsp onion seeds
2 tbsp oil
2 tbsp warm milk
200g self-raising flour
1 tsp baking powder
½ tsp coriander powder
2 tbsp yogurt
3 tbsp butter
1 tbsp sliced garlic
¼ tsp salt
1 tbsp finely sliced coriander leaves

1. In a jug, mix together the hot water, 1 tsp salt, sugar, onion seeds, oil and milk then put to one side.

2. Sieve the flour, baking powder and coriander powder into a large bowl.

3. Add the yoghurt to the dry ingredients. Use a hand mixer to whisk together, gradually adding the hot water mix. Once the dough starts to form, stop adding the water mixture. It should be a soft to the touch dough which is easily pliable.

4. Knead the dough for 10 minutes and then cover with a wet teacloth before leaving to rest for 2 to 3 hours.

5. Mix the butter, garlic, ¼ tsp of salt and the coriander leaves in a bowl and put to one side.

6. When you're ready to bake your naans, pre-heat your oven to 180°C, 350°F, or gas mark 4.

7. Knead the dough again. Take a medium hand sized ball and roll it out into a circular chapatti shape. Repeat until you have used all the mixture.

8. Place it onto a greased baking tray and cook for around 10 minutes. Turn the breads over halfway through cooking.

9. Once cooked, brush the top of the naan with the garlic, coriander oil and place under the grill for a further 2 to 3 minutes.

10. That's it, they're ready – enjoy with curry, kebabs or with dips!

Sweets & desserts

These are an often overlooked part of Indian cuisine – but they shouldn't be! Try rounding off your meal with these easy drinks and desserts. The variety of desserts offered in India is mindboggling, and it's all too tempting to overindulge during festival season. These are my versions of our family favourites. Time to grab a spoon…

Mango kulfi

I make this all the time in the summer – it's the perfect cooling dessert for hot days. The colour will change depending upon which type of mangoes you use; I like to make this with Kesar and Alphonso mangoes, which give a pale yellow colour to your dessert. I make these in kulfi moulds, but if you don't have any, use an ice lolly mould or simply disposable cups.

2 tbsp caster sugar
2 tsp hot water
Pinch of saffron
200g Kesar / Alfonso mango pulp
1 tsp cardamom powder
100g full fat milk powder
1 tsp cardamom powder
Crushed pistachios, crushed almonds, melted chocolate to garnish

1. In a jug, mix the sugar with the hot water, stirring until dissolved.

2. Then add a pinch of saffron and put the mixture to one side to rest.

3. In a blender, whizz the mango pulp, milk powder, cardamom powder until smooth.

4. Once blended, add the sugar mixture into the blender whizz again until fully mixed, then pour into your moulds.

5. Freeze for 2-3 hours until set but still soft.

6. Take the mixture out of the freezer and add the wooden sticks into each mould and return the kulfi to the freezer for a further 5 hours.

7. When you're ready to serve these, remove the kulfi from freezer. Dip the moulds in hot water to release the kulfi, sliding it carefully out of its mould.

8. Once you have removed the kulfi from the moulds you can garnish them `with whatever you choose.

Spiced chai loaf cake

200g unsalted butter
200g caster sugar
200g plain flour
8 cardamom pods, seeds removed and crushed
1 tsp crushed fennel seeds
3 large eggs
1 tsp baking powder
A pinch of salt
A pinch of ginger powder
30 l sour cream
½ tsp rose essence
1 tsp hot water

1. Start by pre-heating your oven to 180°C, 350°F, or gas mark 4.

2. Grease a loaf tin with butter.

3. Cream the butter and sugar together until light in colour. Add the eggs in slowly and blend until incorporated. Add the cardamom seeds, fennel seed, rose essence, ginger powder and sour cream. Whisk until thoroughly mixed in.

4. Sieve the flour, salt and baking powder into the mixture and fold in. Fold in one tsp of hot water.

5. Place the mixture into the greased loaf tin, pop it in the oven and bake for 45-50 minutes.

6. When the timer goes, test the cake with a clean skewer to see it comes out clean. If so, the cake is ready.

7. Remove the cake from the oven and leave to cool on a cake rack until fully cool.

8. This is best enjoyed warm, served with some custard.

My chai

A good cup of chai holds a special place in my heart. So many memories are wrapped up in a single steaming cup; it's seen me through thick and thin, laughter and tears. When you need a hug in a mug – this is what to make, as the spices in the tea gently warm you up from the inside out.

As a cup of chai is so personal, everyone has their own way to make it. I still prefer the version below, as this is the one I grew up with. In India, it can be more milky and heavier, however I love just enjoying the flavour as opposed to being overpowered by the milk. As time goes on you will find your own balance – but this is the way I make it. I find it easiest to use the mug I'm going to serve it in for my measurements, I'd suggest you do the same.

Serves 2-3 people

2 mugs of water
1 inch fresh ginger
½ tsp powdered fennel seeds
1 tsp crushed cardamom
2 teabags
½ mug of milk
Sugar to taste

1. Add the water, ginger, fennel powder and cardamom to a large heavy based pan and bring to the boil.

2. Reduce the heat to a gentle simmer and add the tea bags. Allow to simmer for 2 to 3 minutes before adding the milk and bringing back to the boil.

3. Reduce the heat and allow to simmer for a further 2 minutes, staying nearby to make sure that it does not boil over.

4. After two minutes, use a strainer to strain the tea into the mugs before adding sugar to taste.

Lemon soda

1 tbsp hot water
4 tbsp brown sugar
2 tbsp roughly sliced mint leaves
Juice of 2 lemons
1 tsp cumin powder
1 tsp chaat masala
½ tsp black salt
1 tbsp ginger juice, made from squeezing out the juice from sliced fresh ginger
1l soda water

1. In a large jug, mix the hot water and sugar, stirring until dissolved.

2. Add the mint leaves, cumin powder, chaat masala, black salt, ginger juice and lemon juice into the jug and mix thoroughly. Pour the soda water into the jug and gently mix.

3. Serve over ice and enjoy.

Lassi

Lassis are ubiquitous in India, and there are many different combinations and flavours.

500g plain yogurt
175ml full fat milk
50ml water
50ml hot water
100g caster sugar
2 tbsp thick cream
2 tsp rose water
50 ml buttermilk
1 tsp cardamom powder
Saffron pinch
1 tbsp of crushed pistachios

1. Whizz the yogurt, milk, thick cream and rose water in a blender.

2. In a separate cup, add the sugar to the hot water, stirring until dissolved.

3. Add the sugar solution into the yogurt mix, and pulse until incorporated.

4. Now add the rest of water slowly. How much you'll need depends on how thick you want your lassi. Stop when you have reached your desired consistency.

5. Whisk the mixture all again until it starts frothing.

6. Serve over ice, garnished with saffron and crushed pistachios.

Index

Printed in the United States
By Bookmasters